Welcome to your Mindle

MW01534196

Coloring is more than just a creative activity—it can be a meditative practice, a way to step out of the constant stream of thoughts and into a place of embodied presence.

As a Mindfulness Meditation teacher, I understand how much time we spend caught in our thoughts. What is the quality of yours right now? Are they loud or scattered? Through coloring, we can begin to turn down that mental noise, allowing the soothing act of filling the page with color to guide us. Feel the movement of your hand, notice the softening of your breath, and let yourself slow down.

Each "mind-less" prompt in this book is designed to help you move away from overthinking and into a state of embodiment, finding balance as you release stress and ease into the colorful moment.

May these pages bring you comfort and peace.

Erica Skone-Rees

Certified Mindfulness Meditation Teacher

www.WovenPathWellness.com

Mind-less Moment

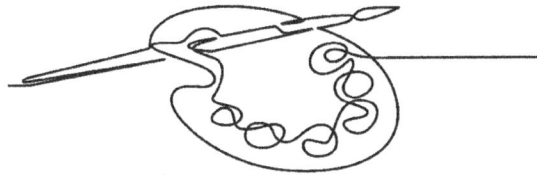

Playful Palette

As you color, give yourself permission to use colors in unexpected and unconventional ways. Pick a hue that you normally wouldn't use for a particular flower or mix colors that traditionally don't match. Let your intuition guide you, and remember, this is a place to play.

Play and unconventional thinking are linked to enhanced creativity and mental agility. This kind of exploration stimulates the brain, fostering cognitive flexibility and psychological resilience. By allowing yourself to experiment freely, you not only boost your creative expression but also enhance your overall well-being.

Mind-less Moment

Soft Hands, Soft Mind

Loosen your grip as you color, letting your hand rest gently around the tool. Let softness flow into your movements and notice how this changes your experience.

This practice allows tension to melt away, calming both your body and mind.

Mind-less Moment

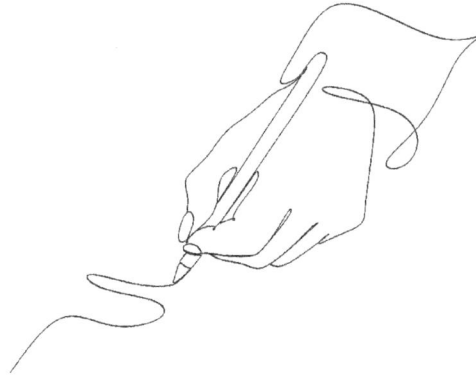

Notice the Pressure

Observe the pressure you apply with your coloring tool. How do different pressures change the outcome?

This awareness can help you become more attuned to your control over situations and your physical responses to stress. Paying attention to how you manipulate the pressure can serve as a metaphor for adjusting your approach in various life scenarios, enhancing your ability to navigate and respond with greater awareness.

Mind-less Moment

Inhale Calm, Exhale Color

With each inhale, fill yourself with calm. With each exhale, let your colors flow onto the page, perfectly paced with your breath.

This technique links relaxation to your creative process, reducing stress and enhancing focus. It transforms your coloring into a meditative act that soothes both mind and body.

Mind-less Moment

Color with a Smile

Invite a gentle smile to the corners of your mouth and allow it to spread softly to your eyes. Feel the lightness in your expression and observe how it influences your mood and your approach to coloring.

Engaging your smile muscles can release endorphins, serotonin, and dopamine, natural mood enhancers that reduce stress and enhance joy. Even a simple, intentional smile, not necessarily genuine, triggers these positive brain effects, enhancing your well-being as you engage in creativity.

Mind-less Moment

The Gift of Gratitude

Pause and take a moment to truly appreciate the time you've dedicated to slowing down. Offer yourself a heartfelt message of gratitude for carving out the time to immerse yourself in this colorful moment. Acknowledge your effort and commitment to self-care.

Practicing gratitude has been scientifically shown to enhance psychological health, reducing stress and promoting happiness.

Mind-less Moment

Use Colors to Reflect Feelings

As you color, choose hues that mirror your current emotions. Select colors intuitively—bright yellows might echo joy, while soft blues could evoke calmness. Pay attention to how these colors align with your feelings, allowing them to express and even transform your emotional state.

Using colors to express emotions can help release their grip, creating space for change or providing a shift simply through acknowledgment and expression.

Mind-less Moment

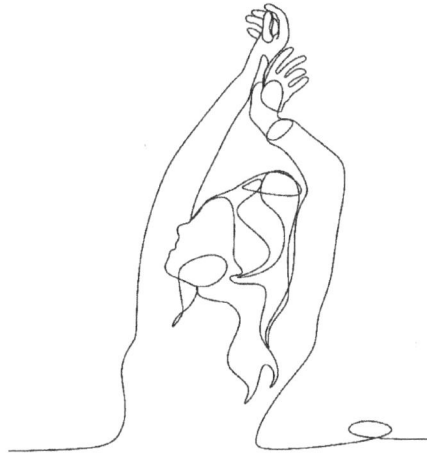

Expand with Each Line

Imagine your lines expanding outward, as though they're radiating from your center. Feel your body opening up with each stroke, allowing spaciousness into your mind and heart.

This practice invites a sense of openness and expansion within, helping you release tension and embrace ease.

Mind-less Moment

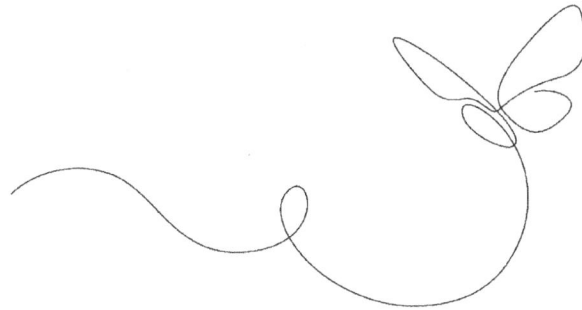

Embrace the Silence

Dedicate a few minutes to color in complete silence, tuning into the gentle scratch of your coloring tool as it moves across the paper.

Coloring in silence helps minimize sensory distractions, allowing you to connect more deeply with yourself and the act of coloring. This quiet focus can calm your mind, enhance your sensory appreciation of the moment, and promote a serene state of being.

Mind-less Moment

Shift and Settle

While coloring, gently adjust your posture or position. Make small, mindful changes—like rolling your shoulders back or stretching your neck. Feel the immediate impact of these adjustments on your body.

This practice enhances spatial awareness and releases physical tension, leading to a more relaxed coloring session. These subtle shifts not only improve circulation but also deepen your connection to your body and the present moment, enriching your mindfulness practice.

Mind-less Moment

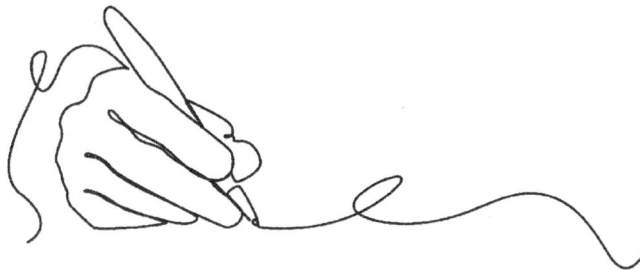

Feel the Weight

As you color, notice the weight of your hand and the tool you're using. Let your hand rest fully on the page as you move, feeling the weight shift with each stroke.

This practice helps you ground into your body, promoting a sense of stability and relaxation.

Mind-less Moment

Breathe in Color

As you select a color, take a deep breath and visualize drawing its energy into your being. Feel the emotion you associate with each color—tranquility with blue, softness with pink, vitality with red, or grounding with green; it's your personal perception that guides the experience.

Color therapy, or chromotherapy, suggests that colors have healing properties. By visualizing these hues flowing through your body, you may tap into their therapeutic benefits, potentially enhancing your mood and health, influenced by either placebo effects or actual physiological changes.

Mind-less Moment

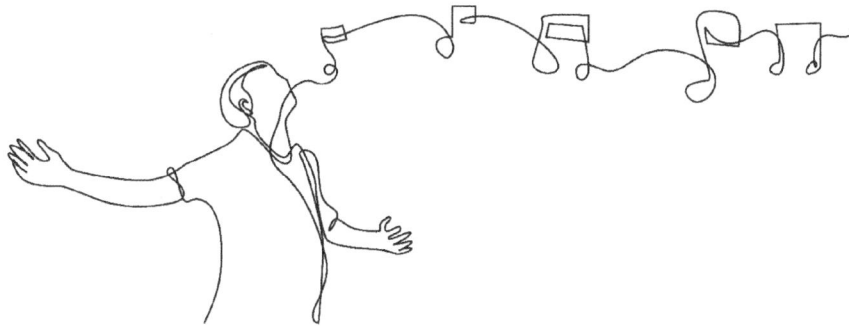

Hum Your Way to Harmony

As you dive into your coloring, incorporate a gentle hum with each exhale, feeling the vibrations resonate like a purring cat. You can choose to hum a familiar tune or simply focus on the natural rhythm of your breath, allowing the hum to flow naturally as you fill in each design.

Humming while coloring engages your auditory senses and tones the vagus nerve, promoting relaxation and reducing stress. This simple act helps focus your mind, decrease anxiety, and deepen your present-moment awareness, enhancing the therapeutic benefits of your coloring session.

Made in the USA
Las Vegas, NV
22 November 2024